Read All About
HORSES

by Nadia Ali

PEBBLE
a capstone imprint

Published by Pebble, an imprint of Capstone
1710 Roe Crest Drive, North Mankato, Minnesota 56003
capstonepub.com

Library of Congress Cataloging-in-Publication Data is available on the Library of Congress website.
ISBN: 9780756572648 (hardcover)
ISBN: 9780756573416 (paperback)
ISBN: 9780756572617 (ebook PDF)

Summary: Did you know that horses can sleep standing up? Or that horses have the largest eyes of any land mammal? Find out all about horses' senses, life cycle, behavior, and more in this fact-filled book.

Image Credits
Capstone Studio: TJ Thoraldson Digital Photography, 1; Getty Images: duncan1890, bottom 6, Robert_Ford, top 7, slowmotiongli, bottom 21, urbancow, top 29; Shutterstock: Alicia Marvin, bottom 18, Alizada Studios, top 4, Alla-B, bottom 11, anakondasp, top 23, Anastasija Popova, middle 26, AnnaElizabeth photography, 15, Bildagentur Zoonar GmbH, bottom 13, middle 25, Budimir Jevtic, top 30, Callipso88, bottom 17, Chursina Viktoriia, bottom 7, Cindy Hughes, bottom 24, Elmari Viljoen, top 25, Erica Hollingshead, 12, Everett Collection, top 6, Hanna Alandi, bottom 25, happylights, top 18, ivanpigozzo, 16, Jackson Stock Photography, bottom 22, Jari Hindstroem, bottom 30, Jemastock, design element, Jirik V, bottom 4, Joseph Sohm, middle 5, Justin Starr Photography, top 26, jvsg9696, bottom Cover, Kelvin Degree, design element,Kwadrat, bottom 5, top Cover, KylieMarie1313, top 21, l i g h t p o e t, top 19, middle 24, L. M. Dunn, middle 27, Makarova Viktoria, bottom 27, mariait, middle 21, Marie-Jamieson, top 5, michelangeloop, 28, NetG, middle 13, nigel baker photography, top 22, Noppanun K background Cover, OlesyaNickolaeva, middle 9, Olga_i, top 9, OryPhotography, 8, pfluegler-photo, top 13, pirita, bottom 9, pirita, bottom 23, Plotitsyna NiNa, top 14, ReVelStockArt, design elements, Rick Haltermann, bottom 10, S.M, top 10, schankz, middle 17, SciePro, bottom 19, Tanhu, 20, Teri and Jackie Soares, bottom 14, Vera Zinkova, top 11, Viktoriia Bondarenko, top 27, Vineyard Perspective, top 17, Volonoff, design element, wavebreakmedia, middle 29

Editorial Credits
Editor: Carrie Sheely; Designer: Bobbie Nuytten; Media Researcher: Donna Metcalf; Production Specialist: Tori Abraham

Printed and bound in China.   PO 5130

Table of Contents

Words in **bold** are in the glossary.

Chapter 1

History of Horses

Horses have lived on Earth for millions of years. Cavemen drew horses on cave walls. Let's learn more about our big four-legged friends.

Scientists believe the earliest horse **ancestor** is a small horse called Eohippus. It lived about 50 million years ago.

All horses belong to the Equus family. Donkeys, mules, and zebras are part of the horse family.

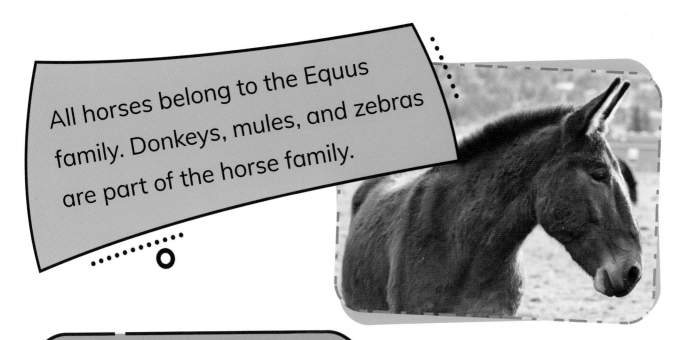

Horses are **mammals**. They breathe air and give birth to live young called **foals**.

People started working with horses more than 5,000 years ago.

There are more than 7.2 million horses in the United States.

Throughout history, people have used horses to get from place to place, to farm, and to hunt.

Horses were used in wars from ancient times to the end of World War II (1939-1945).

In 1860 and 1861, horses of the Pony Express delivered U.S. mail from Missouri to California.

Horses disappeared from North America about 10,000 years ago. Scientists don't know why.

The Przewalski's horse is the only remaining truly wild horse.

Chapter 2

Horse Breeds

Horses come in many **breeds**. Some breeds are very large while others are small. Each one has its own features that make it special.

There are more than 300 breeds of horses in the world.

Arabians are one of the oldest and most prized breeds.

Horse breeds are spilt into five main groups. These are draft horses, gaited horses, light horses, ponies, and warmbloods.

Ponies are small horses. They are usually less than 14.2 hands at the top of the shoulder. Each hand is 4 inches (10 centimeters).

The American quarter horse is one of the most popular breeds in the United States.

Most Appaloosas have a spotted coat pattern.

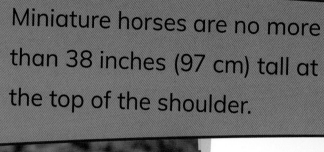

Miniature horses are no more than 38 inches (97 cm) tall at the top of the shoulder.

The shire is one of the largest horse breeds.

Chapter 3

Life Cycle

Horses go through stages of growth. They begin as playful foals and become adult horses. Let's find out how they change and grow.

Horses are pregnant for 11 months.

Females usually give birth to one foal.

Foals can stand one hour after being born.

For six to eight weeks after birth, foals get all of the **nutrients** they need from their mother's milk.

The life stages of a horse include foal, **adolescent**, adult, and senior.

The first year of a horse's life is equal to 6.5 human years.

Foals are very playful. They run and jump.

It takes horses four to five years to reach their adult height.

14

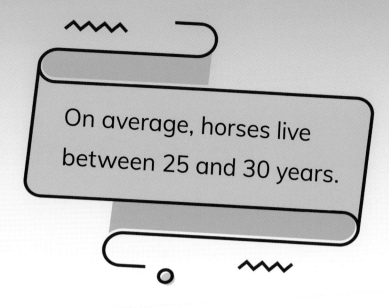

On average, horses live between 25 and 30 years.

Between the ages of 2 and 5, most horses have grown enough to be ridden.

Chapter 4

Horse Bodies

Horses come in different colors and sizes. But they all have similar bodies.

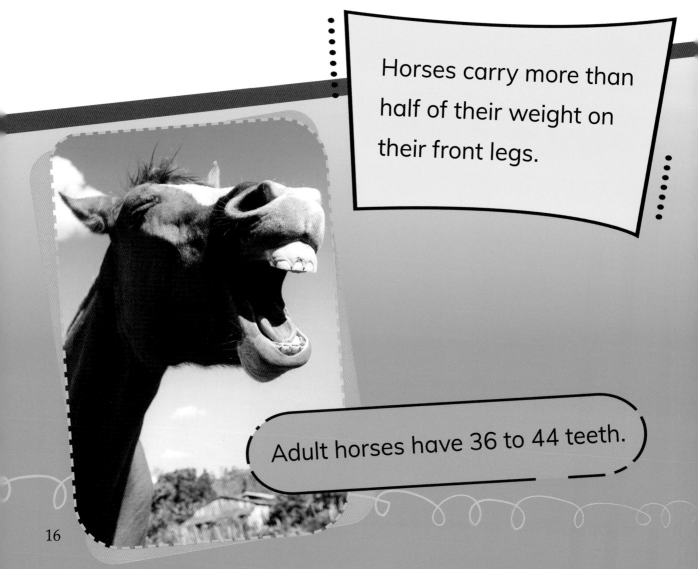

Horses carry more than half of their weight on their front legs.

Adult horses have 36 to 44 teeth.

Many draft horses have long hair on their feet called feathering.

The hard covering at the bottom of a horse's leg is called a **hoof**.

A horse can breathe only through its nose, not its mouth.

Horses have the largest eyes of any land mammal.

Horses can spin their ears in a half circle to focus on a sound.

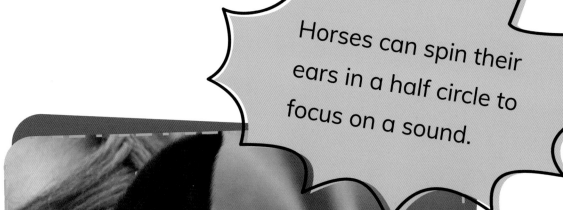

Some horses wear shaped metal horseshoes on the bottom of their hooves. The shoes help protect the hooves.

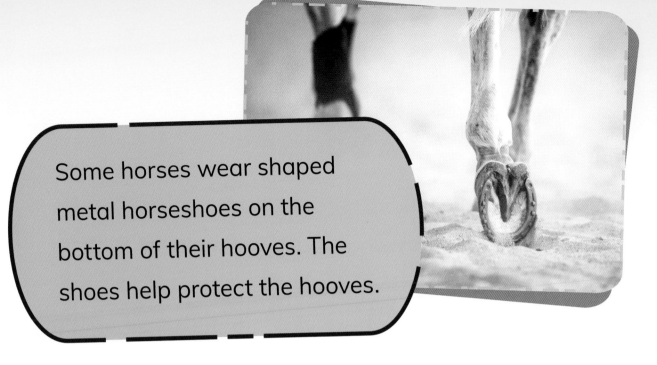

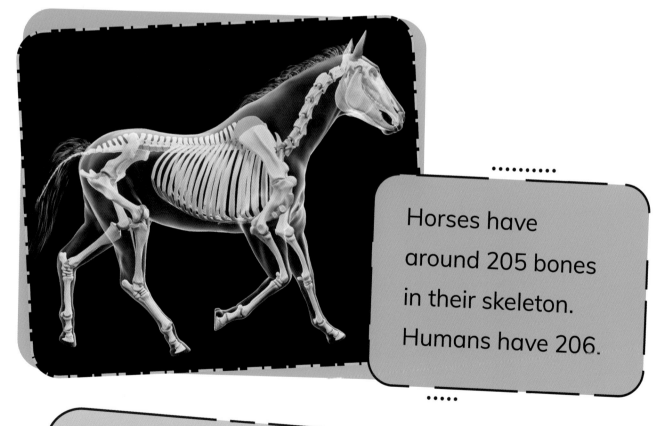

Horses have around 205 bones in their skeleton. Humans have 206.

Horses cannot vomit.

Chapter 5

Senses

Horses have senses that help them understand what is around them. Let's find out how a horse senses the world.

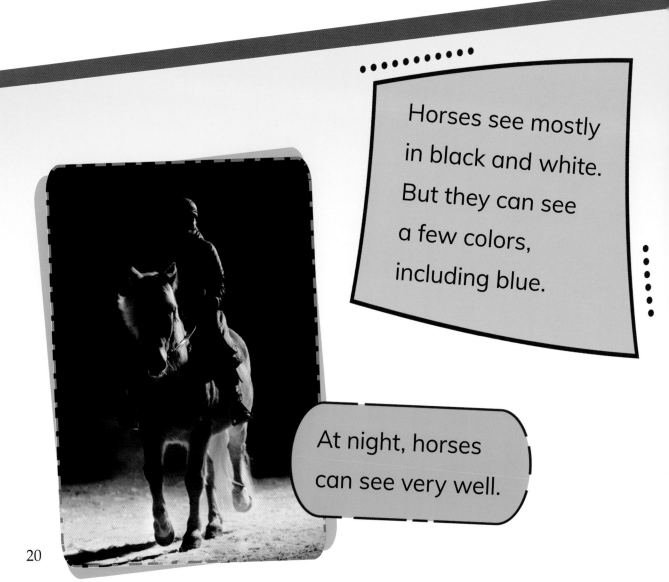

Horses see mostly in black and white. But they can see a few colors, including blue.

At night, horses can see very well.

Horses have a better sense of smell than humans, but not as good as dogs.

Horses can hear sounds too high for human ears.

Horses are **prey** animals. When scared, they naturally want to run away.

Horses have whiskers that are very sensitive to touch.

Horses can see all around, except directly in front of them and straight behind them.

Horses can taste sweet and salty food.

A horse's sense of touch is more sensitive than people's.

23

Chapter 6

Horse Behavior

Horses show many behaviors. You can watch their behavior to help know how they feel.

Horses rest their head on a person's chest or shoulders to show friendship.

Horses neigh for many reasons. They can be worried, looking for another horse, or saying hello.

Horses can make 17 facial movements.

Horses greet each other nose to nose.

Horses can sleep lying down or standing.

In the wild, horses gather in groups called **herds**.

Horses scratch each other's backs to show they are friends.

In a herd, horses have ranks. The horses with the highest ranks are the leaders.

Young horses chase, leap, and run. This helps make their bones stronger.

A horse that is swishing its tail may be annoyed.

Horses put their ears back when they are angry.

Chapter 7

Caring for Horses

Horses are great fun. Looking after them takes hard work. A horse that is cared for well can live a long, healthy, happy life.

Horses need food and fresh water every day. Horses eat mostly hay and grass.

Horses should exercise for at least 20 to 30 minutes a day.

A horse should be seen by a **veterinarian** once a year.

Horses should have **vaccinations** to help protect them from diseases.

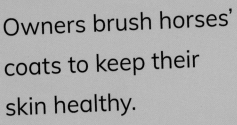

Owners brush horses' coats to keep their skin healthy.

Regular cleaning of stalls helps keep horses healthy.

Glossary

adolescent—a stage of development right before being fully grown; horses are adolescents between the ages of 2 and 3

ancestor—a relative of an existing group of animals that lived a long time ago

breed—a group of animals within a species that share the same features, such as color or markings

foal—a baby horse

herd—a large group of animals that lives or moves together

hoof—the hard covering on a horse's foot

mammal—a warm-blooded animal that breathes air; mammals have hair or fur; female mammals feed milk to their young

nutrient—a substance, such as a vitamin, that animals need for good health

prey—an animal hunted by another animal for food

vaccination—a shot of medicine that protects animals from a disease

Index

About the Author

Nadia Ali is children's book author and a writer. She writes in various genres and is especially fond of animals. Inspired by her kitty, Cici, she contributes pet features to magazines and websites. She was born in London and currently lives in the Caribbean, where she happily swapped out London's gray skies for clear blue skies. She lives with her husband and has two daughters.